T0358707

ON MARCUSE

KEY CRITICAL THINKERS IN EDUCATION

Series Editors:

Michael A. Peters
University of Illinois at Urbana-Champaign, USA

Tina (A.C.) Besley
Calfornia State University, San Bernardino, USA

Scope:

This series is an edition dedicated to the revival of the critical approaches of key thinkers whose thought has strongly influenced and shaped educational theory: Rousseau, Marx, Gramsci, Dewey, Marcuse, Rogers, Freire, Derrida, Foucault, Said and Butler. In this first edition the series includes eleven monographs in total, each approximately sixty pages long with three chapters, a brief introduction, a bibliographical essay, a glossary and series of study questions. The aim is designed to provide cheap and accessible texts for students that give clear accounts of these thinkers and their significance for educational theory. The monographs are written by a group of internationally renown scholars whose own work embodies the critical ethos.

On Marcuse

Critique, Liberation, and Reschooling
in the Radical Pedagogy of Herbert Marcuse

By

Douglas Kellner
University of California at Los Angeles, USA

Tyson E. Lewis
Montclair State University, USA

and

Clayton Pierce
University of Utah, USA

SENSE PUBLISHERS
ROTTERDAM / TAIPEI

A C.I.P. record for this book is available from the Library of Congress.

ISBN 978-90-8790-517-0 (paperback)
ISBN 978-90-8790-518-xx (hardback)
ISBN 978-90-8790-519-4 (e-book)

Published by: Sense Publishers,
P.O. Box 21858, 3001 AW Rotterdam, The Netherlands
http://www.sensepublishers.com

Printed on acid-free paper

TABLE OF CONTENTS

INTRODUCTION

Philosopher, social theorist, and political activist, Herbert Marcuse gained world renown during the 1960s as a theorist of major transformations within both the structures of social production and reproduction and emergent forms of resistance to domination and repression. His theory of "one-dimensional" society provided critical perspectives on contemporary capitalist and state communist societies, while his notion of the "great refusal" won him renown as a theorist of revolutionary change and "liberation from the affluent society." Consequently, he became one of the most influential intellectuals in the United States during the 1960s and into the 1970s. But what is Marcuse's legacy today? While other critical theorists of his generation have gained a new level of academic cache,[1] Marcuse seems to remain a historical figure locked within the dramas of the sixties.[2] As such, a return to Marcuse, as Angela Davis has pointed out, seems to veer dangerously close to "nostalgia" for a past age (Marcuse, 2005).

In this book, we attempt to show that Marcuse continues to have significant relevance and importance to the contemporary situation concerning education in the advanced, industrial world. With the rise of standardization policies in the sphere of schooling, the steady progress of the "affluent society" in the sphere of western, industrialized economies, the waning of critical and dialectical thinking in the field of philosophy and the social sciences, and finally, the immediate degradation of the environment, Marcuse speaks with clarity to academics, teachers, and activists interested in understanding the complexities of "counter-revolution and revolt" occurring today in a variety of locations and across many domains.

Here we demonstrate Marcuse's sustained concern for education as a sphere for developing radical critique and emancipatory alternatives to the fully administered society. We intend our study to show not only Marcuse's

---

[1] See, for instance, Fredric Jameson's (2000) defense of Theodor Adorno as a philosopher of postmodernism, or the renewed and invigorated interest in Walter Benjamin (Agamben, 1998; Zizek, 2001).

[2] Marianne DeKoven makes a similar observation in her book *Utopia limited: The sixties and the emergence of the postmodern* (Durham: Duke University Press, 2004).

1

relevancy, but also the urgency with which we must evaluate his life and work in light of continuities and transformations within the present system of social relations and institutions.

THE LIFE AND TIMES OF HERBERT MARCUSE

Herbert Marcuse was born July 19, 1898 in Berlin, Germany. The son of Carl Marcuse, a prosperous Jewish merchant, and Gertrud Kreslawsky, daughter of a wealthy German factory owner. Marcuse had a typical upper-middle class Jewish life during the first two decades of the twentieth century, in which anti-semitism was not overt in Germany. Marcuse studied in the Mommsen Gymnasium in Berlin prior to World War I and served with the German army in the war. Transferring to Berlin early in 1918, he participated in the German Revolution that drove Kaiser Wilhelm II out of Germany and established a Social Democratic government.

After demobilization, Marcuse went to Freiburg to pursue his studies and received a Ph.D. in literature in 1922 for a dissertation on *The German Artist-Novel*. After a short career as a bookseller in Berlin, Marcuse returned to Freiburg and in 1928 began studying philosophy with Martin Heidegger, then one of the most significant thinkers in Germany.

In his first published articles, written from 1928-1933 when he was studying with Heidegger in Freiburg, Marcuse developed a synthesis of phenomenology, existentialism, and Marxism, anticipating a project which decades later would be carried out by various "existential" and "phenomenological" Marxists, such as Jean-Paul Sartre and Maurice Merleau-Ponty, as well as others in Eastern Europe and the United States in the post-war period. Marcuse contended that Marxist thought had deteriorated into a rigid orthodoxy and needed concrete "phenomenological" experience of contemporary social conditions to update and enliven Marxian theory, which had neglected social, cultural, and psychological factors in favor of economic and political conditions. He also believed that Marxism neglected the problem of the individual and throughout his life was concerned with personal liberation and happiness, in addition to social transformation.

Marcuse published the first major review in 1932 of Marx's previously unprinted early work, the "Economic and Philosophical Manuscripts of 1844", anticipating the later tendency to revise interpretations of Marxism from the standpoint of the works of the early Marx. Marcuse was thus one of the first to see the importance of the philosophical perspectives of the early Marx on labor, human nature, and alienation which he thought were necessary to give concrete substance to Marxism. At the same time that he was writing essays synthesizing Marxism and phenomenology, Marcuse completed a study of Hegel's *Ontology and Theory of Historicity* (1932) which he intended as a "Habilitation" dissertation that would gain him University employment. The text stressed the importance of the categories of life and history in Hegel and contributed to the revival of interest in Hegel that was taking place in Europe.

In 1933, Marcuse joined the Institut fur Sozialforschung (Institute for Social Research) in Frankfurt and became one of the most active participants in their interdisciplinary projects (see Kellner, 1989; Wiggershaus, 1994). The Institute was founded in Frankfurt, Germany, during the 1920s as the first Marxist-oriented research institute in Europe. It developed a conception of critical social theory that they contrasted with "traditional theory." Their distinctive brand of "critical theory" combined philosophy, social theory, economics, cultural criticism, psychology, radical pedagogy, and other disciplines in an attempt to develop a theory of the present age in a dialectic of domination and emancipation. This project involved developing analyses of the new stage of state and monopoly capitalism, of the role of mass communication and culture, of the decline of the individual, of the institutions and effects of German fascism, and of the role of institutions like the corporation, state, media, and schools in the reproduction of contemporary capitalist societies. Marcuse participated in all of these projects and was one of the central and most productive members in the Institute. He deeply identified with the work of the Institute, and throughout his life was close to Max Horkheimer, T.W. Adorno, Leo Lowenthal, Franz Neumann, and its other members.

In 1934, Marcuse – a Jew and radical – and other members of the Frankfurt School fled from Nazism and emigrated to the United States. The Institute was granted offices and an academic affiliation with Columbia University, where Marcuse worked during the 1930s and early 1940s. His first major work in English, *Reason and Revolution* (1941), introduced the ideas of Hegel, Marx, and German social theory to an English-speaking audience. Marcuse demonstrated the similarities between Hegel and Marx, and argued for discontinuities between Hegel's philosophy of the state and German fascism, placing Hegel instead in a liberal constitutional tradition politically and theoretically as a precursor of critical social theory.

In December 1942, Marcuse joined the Office of War Information as a senior analyst in the Bureau of Intelligence (Kellner, 1998). He prepared a report that proposed ways that the mass media of the allied countries could present images of German fascism. In March 1943, Marcuse transferred to the Office of Strategic Services (OSS), working until the end of the war in the Research and Analysis Division of the Central European Branch. Marcuse and his colleagues wrote reports attempting to identify Nazi and anti-Nazi groups and individuals in Germany and drafted a "Civil Affairs Handbook" that dealt with denazification (see the texts collected in Marcuse, 1998). In September 1945, he moved over to the State Department after the dissolution of the OSS, becoming head of the Central European bureau, and remained there until 1951 when he left Government service, following the death of his first wife Sophie Wertheim Marcuse.

After working for the U.S. government for almost ten years, Marcuse returned to university life. He received a Rockefeller Foundation grant to study Soviet Marxism, lecturing on the topic at Columbia during 1952-1953 and Harvard from 1954-1955. At the same time, he was intensely studying Freud and published *Eros and Civilization* (1955), a philosophical synthesis of Marx and Freud which used Freud's categories to provide a critique of bourgeois society and to sketch the outlines of a non-repressive society. The book was well-received and anticipated many of the values of the 1960s counterculture, helping to make Marcuse a major intellectual and political force during that turbulent decade.

In 1955, Marcuse married his second wife, Inge Werner Marcuse, the widow of his friend Franz Neumann who had died in an automobile crash the year before. In 1958, Marcuse received a tenured position at Brandeis University and the same year published a critical study of the Soviet Union (*Soviet Marxism*) which broke the taboo in his circles against speaking critically of the USSR and Soviet communism. Stressing the differences between the Marxian theory and the Soviet version of Marxism, Marcuse provided a sharp critique of Soviet bureaucracy, culture, values, and system. Yet he also distanced himself from those who believed Soviet communism to be incapable of reform and democratization, and pointed to potential "liberalizing trends" which countered the Stalinist bureaucracy and that indeed eventually materialized, leading, however, to the collapse of the Soviet Union in the late 1980s.

At Brandeis, Marcuse became one of the most popular and influential members of its faculty and spoke out frequently on public issues like the Cuban missile crisis, the war in Vietnam, and issues of local importance, as well as teaching and writing. In 1964, Marcuse published *One-Dimensional Man*, which is perhaps his most important work. In 1965, Brandeis refused to renew his teaching contract and Marcuse soon after received a position at the University of California San Diego where he remained until his retirement in the 1970s. Throughout the 1960s, Marcuse supported demands for revolutionary change and defended the new, emerging forces of radical opposition, thus winning him the hatred of mainstream academics and conservatives as well as the respect of the new radicals. In a series of pivotal books and articles, Marcuse articulated New Left politics and critiques of capitalist societies, including "Repressive Tolerance" (1965), *An Essay on Liberation* (1969), *Five Lectures* (1970), and *Counter-revolution and Revolt* (1972). During this time, Marcuse achieved world renown as "the guru of the New Left," giving lectures and advice to student radicals all over the world. His work was often discussed in the mass media, and he became one of the few American intellectuals to gain such attention. A charismatic teacher, Marcuse's students began to gain academic positions and further promoted his ideas, thus contributing to his importance.

After the death of his second wife, Inge Werner Marcuse in 1974, he married his third wife, Erica Sherover Marcuse, on June 21, 1976. Following the collapse of the New Left, Marcuse focused intensely on aesthetics, and his final book, *The Aesthetic Dimension* (1979), contains a defense of the emancipatory potential of art. Marcuse undertook one last trip to Germany where he lectured on topics such as the holocaust, ecology, technology and science, and the fate of the Left; he suffered a severe heart attack and died in Starnberg on July 29, 1979.

Since his death, Marcuse's influence has waned, surpassed, perhaps, by his Institute colleagues Adorno and Benjamin and the emergence of new modes of thinking, such as those found in poststructuralist and postmodern theory. World renown during the 1960s as a theorist of revolution, it is perhaps as a philosopher and social theorist that Marcuse remains an important intellectual figure. Accordingly, in this book we focus on his relevance for the critique and reconstruction of education and present Marcuse as a theorist who attempted to develop a synthesis of philosophy, critical social theory, political activism, and radical pedagogy in specific historical conjunctures. We focus on delineating what we take to be the contributions, limitations, and enduring legacy of Marcuse's work for the transformation of education and society.

CHAPTER ONE SUMMARY

Herbert Marcuse was born to a middle-class Jewish family in Berlin in 1898. As an intellectual, he lived through one of the most dramatic and important moments in Western History, fighting in World War I, experiencing the turmoil of Weimar Germany and rise of German fascism. In 1933 he joined the influential Institute for Social Research in Frankfurt German. Only one year later, he was forced to immigrate to the United States to escape Nazi oppression. In the U.S., Marcuse worked for the United States government on a variety of studies focusing on the origin and nature of German fascism and "denazification" projects for the post-War period. Later as a professor at Brandeis University and then University of California San Diego, he gained renown across the world as the "guru" of the New Left because of his support of student activism and a variety of global protest movements. Due to his activism, Marcuse influenced radical thought and a variety of counter-cultural movements that took place during the 1960s and 1970s in the United States. There was not a more important Leftist thinker in the United States (and perhaps the world) working within this important period of recent history.

CHAPTER ONE QUESTIONS

1) What is the relationship between history and philosophy? What historical events do you think affected Marcuse's philosophy?

2) How has your personal biography affected your beliefs and your intellectual aspirations?

3) According to Marcuse, what impact could philosophy have on combating political, social, and economic forms of oppression?

MARCUSE'S CRITIQUE OF EDUCATION AND SOCIETY

Herbert Marcuse became globally recognized as a radical critic of advanced industrial societies, capitalist and communist, in the 1960s. His book *One Dimensional Man* (1964) carried out a systematic critical analysis of methods of social control and domination generated by the economy, state, culture, and institutions such as school. In this chapter we will outline Marcuse's critique of schooling in relation to his overall theory of one-dimensional society.

An introduction to Marcuse's philosophy of education should be situated in relation to the German romantic philosophical term *Bildung*, which refers to the growth, development, and formation of human beings. *Bildung* aims at autonomous learning/self-formation which concerns the whole individual for the purpose of liberating the self and society (Beiser, 2004).[3] This central ideal remains antithetical to any sense of standardization in education and instead embraces education of the body and mind against passive skill acquisition. Such a philosophic understanding of education was held throughout Marcuse's philosophy: "Once upon a time, it was the proclaimed principle of great bourgeois philosophy that the youth 'ought to be educated not for the present but for a better future condition of the human race, that is, for the idea of humanity.' Now the council for Higher Education is called upon to study the 'detailed needs' of the established society so that the colleges know 'what kinds of graduates to produce'" (1972, p. 27). Here Marcuse criticizes education for the status quo and defends a notion of *Bildung* associated with cultural and social transformation.

Marcuse builds his theory of education from a basic contradiction between *Bildung* as the cultivation of fully developed individuality and

---

[3] The German concept of *Bildung* is one that is also influenced by the ancient Greek notion of *Paideia. Paideia* as a concept and historical idea emphasizes the importance of education as a general cultural spirit that strives to expand and enrich humanity's knowledge in a way that promotes growth and rational modes of life. See Werner Jaeger's three-volume work *Paideia* (New York: Oxford University Press, 1965 [1939]).

what he would famously describe as "one-dimensional man" and society. One-dimensional society is a society that lacks negativity, critique, and transformative practice. It is a society without opposition. Citing trends toward conformity, Marcuse describes one-dimensional society as creating "false" consumer needs that integrate individuals into the existing system of production and consumption via mass media, advertising, industrial management, and uncritical modes of thought. In other words, current society and culture are purely "affirmative," legitimating the on-going existence of material poverty, injustice, and inequality (Marcuse, 1968). Thus affirmative culture is for Marcuse a conservative formation resisting any attempt to negate the social whole in the name of radical transformation. Because affirmative thought justifies the status quo, Marcuse's philosophy of liberation can be described as largely critical and negative. According to Marcuse, negativity is a positive concept in that only through the negation of social contradictions can conformity and oppression be overcome and real freedom and individuality realized. The historical loci for negativity were located on three interlocking registers that included (a) the anthropological level (human faculties of analysis, critique, and imaginative alternatives to the present); (b) the philosophical level (critical concepts that analyze the contradictions of existing conditions); and (c) the political level (individual and social rebellion). Yet within one-dimensional society, these spaces of resistance are, for Marcuse, being eroded at an alarming rate as negativity has given way to uncritical affirmation of the existing society.

(A) ONE-DIMENSIONAL MAN

In terms of the anthropological dimension, industrial society affects every aspect of mind and body, from our intellectual faculties to our libidinal drives. At its inception, factory production had a tendency to repress pleasure. This repression created a libidinal tension between the harsh and brutal demands of work and the need for a fulfilling sensual life, or to use Marcuse's language, a tension between the performance principle and the pleasure principle. The performance principle is a historical manifestation of Freud's reality principle emphasizing competition for scarce resources within a society organized according to the economic performance of workers and capitalists (Marcuse, 1955, p. 44).

In early industrial society, the need to perform labor in appalling factory conditions forced the pleasure principle to be repressed resulting in a condition in which workers were alienated from their own sensual being (creating a working body over and above a body of pleasure). Child labor and unregulated workdays, for instance, were commonplace labor practices in industrial society. These everyday examples of life in industrial society reflect a repetitive, dulling, and mutilating mode of life that Marcuse saw advanced industrial society's technological achievements accelerating. Such a state of alienation and misery according to Marcuse is to be lamented, yet nevertheless, it opened up a space for critique against repressive structures, which were overtly recognized as antagonistic to one's instinctual gratification.

Now in one-dimensional society, the sensual needs of desire, pleasure, and play seem to coincide with a world of commodities that creates a new biological foundation in our sensual and instinctual structures through a more advanced form of capitalism. In other words, the pleasure principle is superficially satiated by the very society that is in fact responsible for the on-going degradation of real, vital needs. Sensuality, according to Marcuse, thus begins to loose its oppositional and liberatory quality, and the "freedom" and "sexual liberty" unleashed within the affluent society are literally "transforming the earth into hell" under the guise of happiness and heaven (Marcuse, 1955, p. xiii).

On the level of behavioral dispositions, the unhappy consciousness of negativity, alienation, and critique is replaced with a "happy consciousness" (Marcuse, 1964, p. 79) which accepts the given as an absolute and undeniable good.[4] Happy consciousness signifies the loss of critical thought that is accompanied by a simultaneous liquidation of potential sources of opposition to established society that are available to individuals such as the media, every day language, and aesthetic representations (music, popular literature, film, music, etc.). Most popular music, for example, is not only a mode of entertainment and marketing but is also political in that it urges conformity to contemporary standards of beauty, reason, and social norms. Thus an inherent claim in Marcuse's concept of the happy consciousness is that cultural activities and practices that cultivate the critical capacities of individuals and communities have

---

[4] The happy consciousness is a concept that Marcuse developed by recalibrating Hegel's famous notion of the unhappy consciousness. In Hegel's *Phenomenology of Spirit* the unhappy consciousness is a distinct phase of thought that develops within the odyssey of human consciousness in history where human identity is paralyzed through its own growth and education. Despite achieving a new level of knowledge of reality, the unhappy consciousness fails to achieve a greater, reconciliatory relationship with reality. Drawing on Hegel's construct of the unhappy consciousness, Marcuse's happy consciousness retains the same symptom of paralysis of educational striving yet with an important difference: instead of a sense of incompleteness, the happy consciousness is a pacified mode of thought that is content with its material and historical situation.

been absorbed into the totality of a hyper consumptive form of capitalism. For Marcuse, then, it is not just that consumer culture has assimilated potentially oppositional realms of culture but also that these forms of negative and critical thought have been replaced with an operationalized way of thinking and attendant sets of values: consumer attitudes and behavior, increasing conformity to market logics, and a complacency to global militarization.

Marcuse further rewrites Freud's psychoanalytic theory by historicizing the Oedipal complex. For Freud, our basic psychological disposition is formed through our early childhood experiences with our parents. For example, young boys enter into an ambivalent relationship with their fathers, who interrupt the sensual pleasures gained from the mother (breast feeding here is key). The resulting Oedipal drama creates a certain critical perspective on the authority of the father, who is both loved and also hated. On a personal and private level, the Oedipal drama crystallizes the more general and public tensions between individual needs and the socially and economically driven performance principle. As such, the Oedipal drama develops the forms of submissiveness and rebelliousness that characterize our struggles in later life, providing a "semi-autonomous" sphere to develop resistance to one-dimensional, administered society.

Yet in advanced capitalism, the traditional role of the private Oedipal drama is replaced by direct socialization. As Marcuse writes, "The classical psychoanalytic model, in which the father and the father-dominated family was the agent of mental socialization, is being invalidated by society's direct management of the nascent ego through the mass media, school and sport teams, gangs, etc." (1970, p. 47). If one's relationship to society was at one time mediated through the private sphere of the family, now the psychological development of the ego is immediately identified with the social order. The distinction between the individual and the masses becomes increasingly blurred. As such, "The multidimensional dynamic by which the individual attained and sustained his own balance between autonomy and heteronomy, freedom and repression, pleasure and pain, has given way to a one-dimensional static identification of the individual with the others and with the administered reality principle" (Marcuse, 1970, p. 47). The ego no longer has the capacity to resist social messages imposed from the outside, resulting again in the evisceration of the negative (the critical) and the production of one-dimensional thinking. Marcuse worries that the triumph of the happy consciousness produces political nihilism where "people cannot reject the system of domination without rejecting themselves, their own repressive instinctual needs and values" (1969a, p. 17). Latch-key children raised through watching television and playing video games, the predominance of consumer culture in and through advertising (especially in school halls, cafeterias, and streamed in television programming such as Channel One) all demonstrate the on-going relevancy of Marcuse's warnings. This brief sketch demonstrates a new psychological importance of schooling in one-dimensional society, for if psychological development is largely conditioned by public social institutions rather than the private family unit, schools become increasingly responsible for either (a) fostering one-dimensional personalities or (b) fostering critical, multidimensional human beings.

(B) ONE-DIMENSIONAL THOUGHT

Philosophically, dialectical thinking once allowed critical thinkers to generate oppositional concepts that could not be absorbed into the language of one-dimensional, normalized thought. For example, concepts like truth or justice opposed conditions of untruth and injustice. Here the tension between is and ought and particular and universal describe not so much flaws within logic but rather inherent contradictions within society as a whole. Now one-dimensional language incorporates into its very form its own opposition, again erasing the ability to think against the status quo. As Marcuse argues, thought "is purged from that 'negative' which loomed so large at the origins of logic and of philosophic thought – the experience of the denying, deceptive, falsifying power of the established reality. And with the elimination of this experience, the conceptual effort to sustain the tension between 'is' and 'ought,' and to subvert the established universe of discourse in the name of its own truth is likewise eliminated from all thought which is to be objective, exact, and scientific" (Marcuse, 1964, p. 140).

Without negative thought, the latent yet suppressed potential within social reality is lost and the unreason of the present becomes the standard for measuring the reasonableness of philosophic or critically reflective argument. What becomes of thought instead is a one-dimensional means-ends logic. Here the ends are taken for granted, never doubted, and never called into question. The only problem remaining is how to arrange the means to achieve these ends. Such thought is referred to by Marcuse and other members of the Frankfurt School as "instrumental thinking" or "instrumental reason". A good example of such means-ends logic is found in the nuclear arms race where the goal of nuclear dominance is never questioned as a social good. Or, during our own political moment in history, the "war on terror" remains largely an unquestioned good whose means are always legitimated in terms of the proposed ends of "peace" and "democracy" despite utilizing the opposites of these concepts as a means.

(C) ONE-DIMENSIONAL POLITICS

On a political level, class struggle no longer appears to be a guaranteed motor for securing a radical social transformation beyond capitalist exploitation (Marcuse, 1964). In orthodox Marxist thought, class struggle between the exploited working class (proletariat) and the exploiting capitalist class (bourgeoisie) of owners would ultimately lead to the overturning of capitalist social relations. Thus, as Marx and Engels predicted in their early analysis of capitalist society, the very motor driving capitalism would be its ultimate downfall.

Yet, throughout the twentieth century the certainty of the orthodox Marxist position was continually undermined as the working class was "pacified" by affirmative culture and one-dimensional thought. The question for Marcuse became: Who are the social actors capable of embodying emancipatory social transformation? Not only had capitalism integrated the working class, the source of potential revolutionary opposition, but they had developed new techniques of stabilization through state policies and the development of new forms of social control.

Thus Marcuse questioned two of the fundamental postulates of orthodox Marxism: the revolutionary proletariat and the inevitability of capitalist crisis. In contrast with the more extravagant demands of orthodox Marxism, Marcuse championed non-integrated forces of minorities, outsiders, and radical intelligentsia and attempted to nourish oppositional thought and behavior by promoting critical thinking and a general refusal of the aggressive and destructive form of life that advanced capitalist society promoted. Marcuse's endless search for alternatives to the "revolutionary" working class struggle demanded engagement with a wide range of oppositional social movements including feminism, ecological activists, counter-cultural hippie love-ins and sit-ins, student protests, and "third world" liberation movements. Rather than despair over the advancement of capitalism and one-dimensional society, Marcuse was always vigilant in his belief that resistance was possible and continually developing in new configurations. It was philosophy's job to in turn analyze the positive and negative, progressive and conservative potentials of these movements.

(D) ONE-DIMENSIONAL EDUCATION

Positioning schooling in relation to the cultural dominant of one-dimensional society, Marcuse resolutely opposed an educational practice in which the negative is replaced with the positive, and, on the level of behavioral and psychological dispositions, the unhappy consciousness is replaced with a happy consciousness. Comparing one-dimensional schooling (as pure positivity) with *Bildung* (as the critical and reconstructive movement towards future possibility), we can more clearly outline Marcuse's dialectical analysis of schooling.

In a 1968 lecture, Marcuse argues that in a one-dimensional society, schooling has become an increasingly contradictory institution. On the one hand, the economy of advanced industrial societies is defined by unrestricted access and development of knowledge, thus a need for a more robust general education system. Here education promises equality and freedom of information access for all social classes – a free market of ideas and new innovations. On the other hand, there is simultaneously the need to "contain knowledge and reason within the conceptual and value universe of the established society" (Marcuse, 1968c) – a society rife with sexism, classism, and racism. As such, the imperatives of the system necessarily limit the democratic potentialities of general education. This tension is resolved in the expansion of highly commodified and commercialized education (as a form of class-based schooling seen today in corporate universities such as DeVry, University of Phoenix, and other such "digital diploma mills," or selling "education" through computer programs).

For Marcuse values associated with modern science and technology under the forces of advanced industrialization and military scientific research (values such as calculability, transparency of method, strict adherence to observable, ahistorical phenomena, efficiency, predictable outcomes, and falsifiability) have been subsumed into the cultural framework of universities and other institutes of higher learning at the expense of education's more fundamental ethical mandate: the betterment of society in accordance with democratic values. Universities increasingly aid in military and capitalist expansion by cultivating not only intellectual property owned by the military-industrial complex but also – and perhaps most importantly of all – a one-dimensional psychological disposition. In other words, Marcuse's critical theory of education contains an unflinching focus on the role higher education plays in obscuring and sanitizing the growing social and political consequences of a one-dimensional educational system that promotes a happy consciousness incapable of seeing the destruction, poverty, and exploitation upon which the affluent society is based.

As such, "education in sickness" (Marcuse, 1968c) is an anti-educative form of schooling concerned with market and military logic under the guise of democratic expansion. Here Marcuse's theory of one-dimensional society can be articulated with that of Erich Fromm's notion of a sane and insane society (Fromm, 1955). It is through education that one-dimensional thought becomes a sickness in the sense that it ceases to be simply a mode of reason and becomes indoctrination into a *whole way of life* incorporating the conscious, unconscious, and the body into a totalizing system of administration and domination. As education becomes increasingly important to the economy – which needs an educated class of doctors, lawyers, scientists, technicians – education's potentially subversive side is concomitantly put in check, leading to escalating forms of institutional and individual repression. A happy consciousness is actually a sick consciousness that misrecognizes the oppression and destruction of one-dimensional society for a pleasure filled utopia.

Such a state of affairs was for Marcuse becoming more pronounced in the push and pull between the Welfare and the Warfare state in the sixties and seventies, and can be seen today in such policies as a Nation at Risk and its punitive descendent No Child Left Behind, both of which subsume the call for "equal educational opportunities" under the logic of capitalist competition and instrumental, state bureaucracy. Bipartisan policies such as these conflate the language of equality with a Cold War language of global domination through educational standards. In fact, we could argue that the tension which Marcuse felt in the late sixties and early seventies has become increasingly overcome by the rapid evisceration of the Welfare state and the preeminent rise of an absolute Warfare state in which social repression and the decline of a critical public and democratic education is even more acute then in Marcuse's days (see Giroux, 2007). In the wake of the Reagan-Bush administrations, Marcuse would see policies such as NCLB and a "teaching for testing" philosophy as accelerating a political project interested in the elimination of the democratic potentials from public education. Thus, Marcuse becomes a starting point for theorizing trends in education that today have become intensified through one-dimensional standardization and neo-liberal approaches to social needs and public policy.

Although heavily critical of educational institutions within advanced capitalist countries, Marcuse also saw opportunities for rehabilitating schools and returning to a robust notion of *Bildung*. As opposed to other radical leftist thinkers of the time, Marcuse refused to abandon the notion of the democratic potential of the university or of public schooling, and instead of "deschooling" (Illich, [1970] 2002) he argued for "reschooling"

(Marcuse, 1975; Kellner, 2007, p. 234). Indeed, students and institutions of higher learning, for Marcuse, represented agents and sites of growing refusal against one-dimensional society. Thus Marcuse, drawing on the work of German student movement leader Rudi Dutschke, argues for the "long march through the institutions: working against the established institutions while working within them" (1972, p. 55). The long march also emphasizes building counterinstitutions such as alternative media, independent schools, and free universities.[5] Thus reschooling must happen by exerting pressures within existing public institutions to democratize education and by exerting pressures from without in the form of alternative education.

Key to understanding Marcuse's theory of reschooling is his on-going relationship with student activist groups. For Marcuse, the three elements of the long march through the institution include nonauthoritarian pedagogy, political education, and student participation/activism (Marcuse, 1972, p. 56). Although Marcuse has been criticized by other theorists such as his friend and colleague Adorno for uncritically embracing student activism, Marcuse actually took a very dialectical view of student revolt and protest, highlighting progressive and reactionary trends within student groups. For instance, on May 1, 1966, Marcuse was sent a packet of literature on the emerging SDS (Students for a Democratic Society) Radical Education Project which contained a 28 page position paper, outlining goals and objectives, organization of study groups, "subject areas of project work" in the academic disciplines, professions, arts, international education, and social movements, as well as developing "political philosophy, ideology, and strategy" and analysis of "the American reality." While Marcuse, in the undated response published below, indicated a willingness to work with the group, he noted the following criticism:

> Much of your project seems to be based on the assumption that education in the American colleges and universities make all but impossible the development of critical thought. You write that 'The basic education of the universities avoids the issues of fundamental conflict and gives little attention to the seminal thinkers who speak to the politics of our times'... Academic freedom is indeed one of the

---

[5] Here we see how Marcuse might support the Internet as a potentially powerful form of revolt against standardized education. The Internet offers multiple avenues for constructing new collective struggles against global forms of oppression as well as a source of information and knowledge that the corporate controlled media omits or distorts. Yet the Internet also, as Marcuse would no doubt warn, is a site of commercialization and corporate power (Kellner & Kahn, 2005).

few liberties both established and effectively used in this country, even more by the Left than by the Right (1966).

As the material collected in *Marcuse's Challenges to Education* (Kellner, Lewis, Pierce, and Cho, 2008) indicates, Marcuse was deeply interested in critique and reconstruction of education and of discovering how the university could be used as a vehicle of progressive social change. His interventions in radical pedagogy demonstrate not only Marcuse's commitment to reschooling, but also his unwavering commitment to critique. Yet we must set straight two possible misunderstandings. First, while some might argue that Marcuse over-zealously endorsed student movements and thus sided with a naïve hope in a better tomorrow, we can see from exchanges like these that Marcuse never abandoned the project of critical theory even as he advocated activist interventions. Second, although highly critical of the dominant logic of one-dimensional society, Marcuse also saw room for resistance in higher education. The goal of emphasizing one-dimensional thinking is not to deny the possibility of resistance but rather to sharpen our abilities to pinpoint progressive opposition working within yet against the system.

Marcuse's engagement with universities was not limited to just a few large campuses and a few radical student groups. Yet another example of Marcuse's unwavering commitment and hope in the university as a site of resistance and social change is found in a lecture he delivered to an audience at Kent State in 1976 that further illuminates his sustained involvement with higher education. Marcuse's Kent State lecture, discovered in the Marcuse archive, is especially poignant given the deadly history of student protest and police violence that took place at this university in May 1970. In this particular lecture, given in a place where a high price was paid for student resistance to the U.S. troop escalation in Vietnam and military operations in Cambodia, Marcuse reminded the audience that great gains had been made through student protest and resistance to establishment violence and irrationality. Invoking the student and worker general strike of 1968 in Paris, massive anti-Vietnam war protest, and the civil rights movement here in the U.S., Marcuse continued to insist that higher education could be instrumental in individual and widespread cultural and social transformation.

Marcuse's focus in the Kent State lecture aimed at revolutionizing both the subjective and objective conditions of one-dimensional society. In a context of heightened repression and increasing state violence Marcuse offered the following prescriptions for educational change:

Today, under the conditions of repressive integration, the change within individual emancipation may be the task of small education groups, political and psychological in one, practicing self-education, in and against the official education. As political education, the work would to a large extent aim at the demystification and defetishization of Marxism in theory and practice: developing the Marxian concepts in accordance with the conditions of the 20th century conterrevolution. As a psychological education, the work would be focused, not on a nice release of our Ego and Id, of our frustrations, our psyche, but on an autocritique of our psyche: learning to distinguish between needs and satisfactions which are liberating on a social scale, and those that are self-destructive, block liberation, learning to distinguish between behavior which reproduces in ourselves the Establishment (often in the guise of radicalism!), and behavior which is really emancipatory: striving for a morality of liberation which overcomes, in ourselves, the cynical and brutal morality of the Establishment. In short: internal transformation of psychological into political, of therapy into political education (Marcuse, 1976).

Marcuse's point here is not that students should add therapy sessions to their education. What he is suggesting is for students to collectively develop practices of decolonizing the internalized objective reality of one-dimensional society. In other words, Marcuse is arguing that education needs to be politicized at the psychological core of the individual because the repressive and irrational status quo of one-dimensional society has already politicized the subject, official education being a key actor in this process. A happy, one-dimensional psychology has to be overcome through the concerted effort to critique the status quo and resist political co-optation. As such, Marcuse reminds us that liberation must remain anchored in the critical capacity to understand the progressive and conservative tendencies within schools, universities, and student movements.

CHAPTER TWO SUMMARY

In this chapter we situated Marcuse's analysis of schooling in relation to his dialectical critique of society. In the 1960s, Marcuse argued that the major cultural, political, and social obstacle to human freedom was the rise of "one-dimensional society" that grew out of the industrial period. The problem with one-dimensional society is that it resists critique and supports conformity to a hyper-consumptive culture. Additionally, the traditional resources where critique can be developed in individuals have been co-opted and incorporated into a system of administration that links the formation of identity with the needs and desires produced in one-dimensional society. These critical resources include instinctual needs set against exploitative labor, philosophical questioning set against technological language, and political antagonism set against political fatalism. To understand the social role of schools, we have to place them within this broader understanding of one-dimensional society. Only by connecting school life with dominant cultural, political, and psychological trends can we begin to see how schools support one-dimensional thinking and potentially act as institutions to resist such thinking. General education, in other words, can be reconfigured in a way that reflects growth away from a sick and unhealthy society towards one that begins to strive toward social, ecological, and individual health.

CHAPTER TWO QUESTIONS

1) What are the key features of a one-dimensional society? Do you agree with Marcuse that society has become one-dimensional?

2) How has your educational experience proved or disproved Marcuse's critique of schooling as one-dimensional?

3) Drawing inspiration from Marcuse's analysis of student resistance, how can students today fight against one-dimensional education? What about teachers?

4) What does Marcuse mean when he writes "We are again confronted with one of the most vexing aspects of advanced industrial civilization: the rational character of its irrationality" (1964, p. 9)?

5) What is a happy consciousness and do you think that it is still a psychologically dominant disposition today?

6) How do you interpret Marcuse when he argues "I have stressed the key role which universities play in the present period: they can still function as institutions for the training of counter-cadres [revolutionary groups]" (1972, p. 56). In what ways can the university play this role?

MARCUSE'S ALTERNATIVE OR, TOWARD A RADICAL RECONSTRUCTION OF EDUCATION

An education for both social and psychological health requires for Marcuse a radical reconstruction of the curriculum and teaching beyond current day standardization, proficiency testing, and what Paulo Freire (1972) calls "banking education." Out of the reconstruction of education, Marcuse would hope to develop the multidimensional dispositions that characterize *Bildung*, including critical thinking, moral judgment, and political activism or strong civic engagement. Below we will outline the key elements for reconstructing school curricula and then provide a brief description of a multidimensional student.

(A) ART AND THE HUMANITIES

To begin, the humanities should be valued as much as the sciences in order to develop a full notion of human experience. Art, for instance, cultivates the senses, the imagination, and the ethical aspect of reason – fostering a robust notion of *Bildung* and aesthetic self-formation.[6] Art holds open the broken promise of happiness beyond the current affirmative culture and administered society. As Marcuse repeatedly emphasized, aesthetic beauty is a "great refusal" of one-dimensional society and the commodified world of capitalism. In an interview with Richard Kearney, Marcuse succinctly summarizes his notion of aesthetic education: "(1) to negate our present society, (2) to anticipate the trends of future society, (3) to criticize destructive or alienating trends, and (4) to suggest 'images' of creative and unalienating ones" (Kellner 2007, p. 228). In sum, art "negates" the present society by showing its negative features and offers visions of a better

---

[6] Charles Reitz's *Art, Alienation and the Humanities* (2000) highlights the importance of aesthetic education in Marcuse's radical philosophy of education, which he suggests could be combined with critical pedagogy and existing progressive alternative educational projects to help carry through a contemporary reconstruction of education, a project we share.

world. The aesthetic dimension gives form to a new reality principle beyond the limits of the one-dimensional performance principle by anticipating a certain form of "poetic justice" (Marcuse, 1969a, p. 43) in which reality is both indicted for its crimes and redeemed through imaginative reconstruction. Beauty and the aesthetic dimension, in other words, have a radical if not revolutionary function, fostering the development of real, vital, and sensual needs and inspiring action that transcends the present condition.

A key to understanding Marcuse's aesthetic theory is that the truth of art lies in its form not in its specific content. Thus art liberates the senses from the given by creating new aesthetic forms of representation, not through overtly political content. For Marcuse, a cubist painting of a still life is just as political as a photograph of a union strike, because it allows another way of seeing a fragmented and multifaceted world. In fact, it is the autonomy of the cubist still life that for Marcuse reveals art's most political function, in that it radicalizes perception, promoting an alternative vision of reality, rather than just conveying a political message. "In this sense," Marcuse writes, "art is 'art for art's sake' inasmuch as the aesthetic form reveals tabooed and repressed dimensions of reality: aspects of liberation" (1978, p. 19).

The withdrawal of art from taking ideological sides represents art's ultimate refusal of the administered society, expressing a total form of emancipation that, in its political equivalent, would necessitate revolution. While we might be critical of Marcuse's aesthetic formalism here, he does provide an important reminder that art, even at its most abstract, does promote the cultivation of new aesthetic sensibilities which at their root serve as political protest. Love of nature, for instance, can promote ecological vision and action; love for people and sympathy for the oppressed can promote political struggle; and revulsion against brutal repression in the name of beauty can promote hopes and struggles for a more just and peaceful world.

Likewise, his emphasis on the Humanities and philosophy emphasizes the importance of developing critical thinking and the ability to put existing realities in question and envisage alternatives. Marcuse was a philosopher by training who believed in the importance of classical philosophy in developing a critical consciousness. Rather than abandon the "classics" of the liberal arts tradition, Marcuse argued that they were important resources for thinking against the administered society. But this does not mean mere acceptance of the "inherent truth" or "beauty" of the classics. Rather, for the canon of literature and philosophy to retain its transformative potential, these texts have to be read critically and historically. In our current age of standardization in schools and the cutting of arts based education programs and the Humanities, Marcuse's emphasis on the connections between aesthetics, philosophy, critical thinking, and transformative practice is more pressing than ever.

(B) HISTORY

In Marcuse's critical classroom, students would be encouraged to research the history of global struggles against exploitation. Rather than a history from above, one that uncritically celebrates the triumphs of the Western modern project, this would be a history from below: a history of the struggles of the oppressed. Thus a counter-history to imperial domination should be taught – a history that moves the margins to the center and in the process gives possible models for future forms of political dissent. This history should include not simply class struggle (as in a classical Marxian perspective), but also focus on new and emergent forms of struggle including anti-patriarchal and anti-racist resistance.[7] Furthermore, education has the potential to mediate between struggles against exploitation, pinpointing underlying similarities in order to build a coherent counter-hegemonic bloc united in the struggle for freedom and a more socially just world. Here, students might reference *Counterrevolution and Revolt* (1972) as a model for envisioning a new notion of history for social transformation. This book is structured by a critique of domination (the counterrevolution in the Nixon administration), and evocation of individual revolt and emergence of new social movements that continued the struggles of the 1960s. As demonstrated above, Marcuse's radical pedagogy would emphasize how history is a constant struggle between opposing forces in a dialectical movement of liberation and oppression. Instead of focusing on facts, dates, and particular historical figures, history curricula should teach patterns of struggle and domination that have constituted human societies up to the present.

(C) SCIENCE AND TECHNOLOGY STUDIES

Furthermore, science and technology should be rethought in relation to human needs and the social good. Rather than simply commodifying science and technology in the interests of corporations and the military

---

[7] For a further development of Marcuse's theory of racism and race see Calderon in Kellner, Lewis, Pierce, and Cho (2008). For examples of history textbooks that embody the alternative view of history cited here, see for instance Howard Zinn's *People's History of the United States* (1983) or Frantz Fanon's polemic *The Wretched of the Earth* (1980).

industrial complex, technical education has to become politically oriented towards emancipation. A new science and technology for Marcuse would have to begin by "insist([ing]) on the liberation of science from its abuse for exploitation, destruction, and domination" (1975).[8] Marcuse never wavered in his view that science and technology provided the potential to abolish human toil and scarcity. Indeed, in his *One-Dimensional Man*, widely considered his most pessimistic work, Marcuse suggests that an alternative society should begin with an emancipatory reconstruction of science and technology. In other words, Marcuse's critical theory of education presents us with an educational challenge to develop alternatives to late capitalism's co-optation of science. The alternative value set that Marcuse advocates begins with a more humanistic and ecologically healthy perspective, one that focuses on the social and political dimensions of science and technology.

Marcuse's perspective on science and technology education is more relevant today than perhaps at any other time in history. This is because our contemporary educational moment is one that is not only defined by the standards movement and a "teaching-to-the-test" atmosphere, but we are also witnessing a resurgence of a neo-Sputnik movement that is now focusing considerable efforts toward channeling resources, educational focus, and training to science, technology, and math education in a massive campaign to train and prepare students to contribute to the highly dynamic and innovative global economic base. Here, destructive and economically oriented goals become the sole, urgent aim of science and technology education. Such a neo-Sputnik educational push comes at precisely the wrong time, when real public problems such as global climate change, environmental degradation, and human health disasters caused by the unintended consequences of science and technology are prevalent all across the globe.

---

[8] The indictment Marcuse leveled against scientific and technological research that took place within universities, institutes, and think tanks is still a valid one. Contemporary examples include tobacco giant Phillip Morris funding a 6 million dollar research project on "addiction studies" in UCLA's neurological science department; "clean coal technology" developed by the coal industry to "repackage" dirty fuels; biotechnologies that allow genetically altered foods and cancer-producing pesticides to pervade society as well as the natural world. Undoubtedly, the dominant model of science and technology that drives research and funding today is still one that is largely anti-democratic, predicated on "false values" of greed, destruction, and aggression (Beck, 1992; Grim, 2008).

(D) EDUCATION FOR LIBERATION

In sum, all academic subjects need to be restructured towards democratic ends: science cannot be instrumental but must incorporate into it a notion of the public good and social welfare; history should be history of oppression and resistance; sociology must produce knowledge useful to the oppressed; aesthetics should be utilized as a tool for cultivating a new sensuality and for fueling imaginative alternatives to public problems; philosophy should develop the capacity for critical thinking and articulating alternative visions of human life; and economics has to include a political dimension beyond simple mathematical calculation of markets. This orientation is not a rejection of or retreat from the "objectivity" of education, or education as being organically tethered to the empirical conditions of human reality. Rather it is a rejection of the false neutrality supporting objectivity. Such neutrality merely masks the values of one-dimensional society underlying the objectivity of the academy (even the objectivity of the "hard sciences"). Here Marcuse would advocate a "strong objectivity" (Harding, 1998) that is objective precisely because it recognizes the political nature of all knowledge systems and that this political dimension is not so much a stumbling block as it is a source for new political and scientific discovery. Marcuse argues for educational norms based on enhancing political freedoms and democratic sensibilities rather than military domination or capitalist profiteering. As such, Marcuse is not politicizing the curriculum, but rather demonstrating the inherently political nature of teaching and learning.

This model of radical education is distinct from other progressive educational movements. In a speech given at the Immaculate Heart College in 1970, Marcuse was clear that his embrace of counter-education is not simply "learn-when-you-want-to-learn" or "learn-what-you-want-to-learn" as in alternative educational experiments such as Summerhill where students are free to play all day and not attend classes.[9] Rather, reschooling should be concentrated on political liberation, sensual development, and critical reason geared towards overcoming the contradictions of the present. Thus "anarchy" is not an educational virtue for Marcuse, since for him education should be guided towards the realization of the potentials of the student – potentials that only become actualized through the careful co-

---

[9] See Lewis's discussion of play in Kellner, Lewis, Pierce, and Cho (2008); on Friedrich Schiller's analysis, which Marcuse draws upon in his claim for the importance of play for education, see *On the Aesthetic Education of Man* (2004).

construction of the learning environment between the student and teacher in the name of freedom.

Marcuse's radical pedagogy is also different from that of John Dewey. While Dewey and Marcuse would agree on many points, a major point of divergence would be the intensity and the urgency of Marcuse's critique of advanced capitalism and the administered society. Furthermore, Dewey's analysis of science and technology remains uncritical of the scientific method itself as a historical and cultural construct fully implicated in relations of power. Perhaps the closest to Marcuse's educational position would be Paulo Freire and his pedagogy of the oppressed. If Freire provides educators with the pedagogical method for critical-consciousness raising in the form of problem-posing dialogue, then perhaps we can argue that Marcuse provides content for this dialogue, focusing on a reconstruction of curricula. In sum, Marcuse's theory of reschooling is distinct from other educational philosophers, mediating between a "classical" humanities oriented education and the real world political necessities of the historical moment.

Reconstructing the curriculum will help cultivate critical thinking in students. Critical thinking according to Marcuse locates reactionary and fascist tendencies within current political trends – an educational ethic that links Marcuse closely with Adorno's own anti-fascist education. These tendencies include insurgent racism, nationalism, imperialism, militarism, and increases in societal violence and aggression. Thinking against escalating fascism and imperialism is a form of thinking critically and calling into question all seemingly "natural" or normative distinctions between what is considered good or bad by societal standards. In other words, the political economy of societal norms and their historical conditioning should be emphasized. Critique is, for Marcuse, more than simply pealing away layers of lies found in political propaganda (although this is certainly a major component). As he once wrote, "… the Orwellian language is not only a blatant lying contradiction, it is also expressive of the facts. We terminate the war in Indo-China by extending it. We withdraw while invading…It seems to me that here we have, strange as it may seem, the linguistic expression of the real contradictions of capitalism today: it is simply correct that this society can have peace only by preparing for war or even by waging war" (Kellner, 2005, p. 142). That is, the falseness of such statements is a true representation of the falseness of the whole of society, of its inherently contradictory and destructive reality.

Thus dialectical thinking against fascist one-dimensionality includes both an analysis of political dis-information and also – at the higher level of systemic critique – an analysis of how these lies are themselves the truth of one-dimensional society. The political unconscious in other words is not hidden behind a false screen but rather is *hidden in plain sight* in a language that has absorbed into its very form its own opposition (Marcuse, 1964, p. 90). As such, Marcuse's educational mandate to combat fascism is also a search for a language of negation capable of articulating this critique in the first place. Such a language is not simply reducible to an academic language. Rather, Marcuse finds resources for this counter-language in youth culture and in the practices of his students (see the example of Angela Davis below).

Education and teaching have to be infused with an existential component: the need to commit to social struggle for individual and social transformation. Here Marcuse moves from cognition and sensual development towards ethical development and moral and political education in general, and it is with this move that his theory is perhaps most controversial considering the clear rejection of ethics in our instrumental and one-dimensional society. As Horkheimer and Adorno argued in *Dialectic of Enlightenment* (2002), enlightenment has become an instrumental form of reason detached from ethical questions concerning the ends of technological development. As such, Marcuse's existential move towards the choice to fight for freedom against the false needs of one-dimensional society strikes at the very heart of the dialectic of enlightenment itself. The ability to think the negative has to become a form of action that moves towards a transformation of social relations through activism on multiple interconnected fronts.

Ethical education is thus connected with political education and making education relevant to the pressing social and political issues of the day. In an interview with Henrich von Nussman in Germany in 1969, Marcuse explicitly advocated an *"education toward radical change"* (Marcuse 1969b). He believed that this was a key task for students and intellectuals involved in the radical social movements of the 1960s, arguing that:

> The task is education in a new sense. This is an education which does not remain in the classroom or the walls of the university, but an education which spontaneously reaches over into action, into *Praxis,* and which extends to social groups outside of the university … In the universities, for example, a structural reform could be accomplished which would work counter to the technocratic educational system which leads to training rather than education. This can occur by means of increased pressure from student groups within the framework of the already existing universities. I do not see any other way of breaking the domination of false consciousness (Marcuse, 1969b, p. 26).

Political education for Marcuse should help prepare students to engage in acts of civil disobedience against injustice. Civil disobedience demands that what society deems "good" be properly negated as what is in fact "bad" in relation to democracy and personal liberation. Marcuse warns: "True this kind of education may well reduce the protective barriers which separate the classroom from the reality outside. It may promote civil disobedience. It may even be undemocratic in terms of the established democracy" (1968c). Civil disobedience can include many forms. For instance, Marcuse continually emphasized that students should take their education into their own hands and demand that the curriculum change to meet the needs of the "new sensibility." Just as workers must take control of the means of production, so too must students for Marcuse take control of the means of intellectual production: the universities. Thus Marcuse stresses the need for students to struggle for education as a contested terrain, to combat deceptive neutrality of the university, abolish the class character and exclusionary history of access to higher education, and finally to work to unite the struggle for education with a broader liberation front.

Stated simply, Marcuse's educational philosophy is one of health against sickness, and of liberation against domination. For Marcuse, one-dimensional schooling is precisely the tool for passing social sickness down through the generations. It equates education with indoctrination into a one-dimensional world that leaves no room for the revolutionary possibilities of negation. Here knowledge becomes simply "that which is" and to be educated is reduced to conformity to standards of knowledge production and social adjustment. In this context, a Marcusean educational philosophy would reclaim education from the contradictions of the Welfare/Warfare state and promote a pedagogy of health as opposed to a pedagogy of destruction and death. Reschooling in the end calls for a critical analysis of curriculum development and standardized pedagogy guided by the principles of critical thinking, ethical commitment, sensual reconstruction, and individual and social transformation.

The embodiment of a Marcusian multidimensional student/activist is clearly articulated in his description of one of his most well known students, Angela Davis. After having been put in prison for her connections with the radical Marxist George Jackson, Marcuse defended Davis in a 1971 statement where he affirmed that Angela Davis was

... an extraordinary student not only because of her intelligence and her eagerness to learn, to know, but also because she had that sensitivity, that human warmth without which all learning and all knowledge remain "abstract," merely "professional," and eventually irrelevant. Angela learned what the great philosophers were constantly talking about: human freedom, the dignity of man, equality, justice – and how human relationships and human society ought to be based on these ideas. She grasped what every good student will grasp very soon: that great ideas are nothing unless they are more than mere "ideas," mere "values" to be professed in classrooms, in the churches, by the politicians; that they are false and irrelevant unless they are being translated into reality ...

Angela was an excellent teacher – even her critics admitted that she did not use the classroom for propaganda and indoctrination. She did not have to! For presenting the facts, analyzing the prevailing conditions was enough. She refused to treat the liberating ideas of Western civilization as mere textbook material, as stuff for examinations and degrees – for her, they were alive and had to become reality – here and now, not in some far away days, not eternal promises and expectations. So she could not confine herself to the classroom, to the relatively same formation and isolation of the campus: she took the truth (her truth, our truth) outside: she protested, she demonstrated, she organized, and she did not conceal her political affiliations (Marcuse, 1971).

Here we see a clear summary of Marcuse's theory of teaching and learning. For instance, in Angela Davis, Marcuse saw a student that was passionately connected with the subject matter in a deeply personal and political way. Second, as a teacher, Davis was not simply a propagandist for the left– a charge that has been leveled with increasing frequency against professors interested in race, class, and gender inequalities. Rather, it was through a dialectical analysis of the contradictions constitutive in society involving class, race, gender, sexuality, and the mode of production that her critique emerged. Thus, education was not about simply political indoctrination – which would amount to the loss of critical thinking – but rather about a concerted examination of how the formal freedoms of the affluent society and industrial capitalism produce irreconcilable tensions.

Thirdly, Davis drew upon the objective reality that surrounded her as a teacher and citizen which in turn informed her practice in the classroom and the public sphere. Again, utilizing and demanding a stronger concept of objectivity, a fuller account of the ways in which racial, class, gender, and sexual oppression are part of the daily make-up of society and history, Davis' pedagogical model serves as a strong example of rehabilitating objectivity from instrumental frameworks.[10] As a teacher Davis' activities in the classroom and also outside the classroom were fully engaged in political opposition against oppression, not as isolated practices but as an integrated and dialectically connected activity.

For Marcuse, education as activism began to blur lines between the university and the street, expanding the notion of education beyond the constrictions of "schooling." As opposed to Plato who founded the university as a place of seclusion and isolation, Davis thus returned to the Socratic model in which the "university" was located in the streets of the city, and the educator was a public intellectual. Such a move is risky – Davis lost her job at UCLA, and Marcuse, who likewise sided with students in acts of civil disobedience, was heavily criticized and under constant attack and threat of death by the right (Kellner, 2005). Indeed, in terms of historical precedent, Socrates himself lost his life for having such an ethical position. Yet, this ethical commitment was for Marcuse a central tenet of education against one-dimensional thinking and the complacency of the happy consciousness.

The goal of a multidimensional, radical pedagogy, is to enhance the ability to resist the lure of one-dimensional, totally administered society. In other words, reschooling is part of a larger effort to realize what Marcuse often referred to as a "great refusal." The great refusal is a revolutionary denunciation of all that exists and a concomitant commitment to utopian political, social, cultural, and psychic liberation. Interestingly enough, Marcuse also referred to the great refusal as "permanent education" incorporating all facets of social and psychological life, thus linking the great refusal back to the romantic notion of *Bildung* (1969a, p. ix). In terms of the political dimension of resistance, students should engage in civil disobedience (as described above) against militarism, exploitative economic politics, and violations of human freedom. On a cultural level, students should resist immediate identification with society and media culture and instead remember to think critically of images, messages, and consumer propaganda and to question their sources and suggested values. On the political level, teachers and students should attempt to discover the key issues and problems of the day and intervene to help resolve them. And on a psychological level the false needs of the administered society (greed, violence, militarism, etc.) should not be mistaken for our real, genuine needs (which include love, freedom, personal fulfillment, and human and non-human empathy for instance). Even the long march through the

---

[10] On "strong objectivity," see Harding (1998), in particular chapter eight where she lays out what such a concept of objectivity would look like.

institutions must be informed by the great refusal as a normative ideal or utopian horizon that allows us to work within one-dimensional society without having to adopt its logic, values, or sensibilities. Reschooling is a powerful weapon against the "one-dimensional man" and the happy consciousness, and activists and teachers such as Davis provide powerful, inspirational models that realize Marcuse's clarion call for a healthy, multidimensional world.

SUMMARY OF CHAPTER THREE

In this chapter, we argued that Herbert Marcuse's radical reconstruction of education sought a pedagogy of health against sickness, and liberation against domination. This requires aesthetic education and the liberation of the senses; philosophical education that cultivates critical thinking and offers potential alternatives; political education that inverts history's perspective and focuses on social struggles and marginalized peoples; critical studies of science and technology aiming at their reconstruction and the development of a new set of values for technologies that are oriented toward individual and social transformation; and education aiming at the cultivation of the individual and social transformation rather than social reproduction.

Marcuse connected reconstructions of education with social activism rooted in the objective conditions of late capitalist society. For Marcuse the dialectical relationship between the world created through an imperial and predatory form of capitalism and engaged struggle against such conditions is the material in which a liberatory education and society should be founded. Drawing upon this more empirically accurate reality instead of the one promoted and distorted through one-dimensional modes of cultural production is one of Marcuse's most powerful legacies for rethinking educational thought and practice.

QUESTIONS FOR CHAPTER THREE

1) How will you teach students to be multidimensional individuals? Give examples from your specific disciplines and design lesson plans that embody Marcuse's ideas.

2) How do you interpret Marcuse's suggestion that individuals embody a sense of "great refusal" to one-dimensional society? Does he mean that individuals in one-dimensional society should move "off the grid" and disengage from society in general?

3) Do you agree when Marcuse argues "All authentic education is political education" (1972, p. 47)? In other words is neutrality possible in teaching? And even if it is possible, is it desirable?

4) If education for health against sickness cultivates real, vital needs over and against false needs of the administered society, who decides what these needs are? And if we can define these needs, how can teachers in their classrooms foster real, vital needs by reconstructing their curricula?

5) Can or should political and social controversies be sources for developing critical thinking in classrooms? What challenges to incorporating such a teaching model can you anticipate and how would you overcome these challenges?

MARCUSE'S LEGACY

A return to Herbert Marcuse is thus not at all a nostalgic wish but is an urgent and necessary theoretical and political move at this historical moment. Although the world has changed significantly since the sixties, many of these changes are not fundamental ruptures with the past but rather intensifications of trends that Marcuse was keenly aware of. One-dimensional thinking, increasing standardization of social relations and of knowledge, and the colonization of education by capitalist and military interests are all germane for understanding our postmodern, globalized world. We can thus turn to Marcuse's work as a model embodying a broad, critical perspective necessary to capture the major socio-historical, political, and cultural features of the day. Such attempts to get at the Big Picture, to theorize the fundamental changes, developments, contradictions, and struggles of the moment are desperately needed in an era of globalization whose dizzying complexity in many ways resists totalization. Marcuse's thought thus continues to be relevant because he provides a mode of global theoretical analysis, allowing educators and students to map the intricate interconnections between macro-shifts on a global stage and micro-shifts in educational policy and reform.

Marcuse also provides comprehensive philosophical perspectives on domination and liberation that are important today for educators concerned with teaching against one-dimensional thinking and the happy consciousness. In retrospect, Marcuse's vision of liberation – of the full development of the individual in a non-repressive society (*Bildung*) – distinguishes his work as a dialectical balance between ardent critique and utopian aspirations for radical transformation. Thus, we believe that Marcuse overcomes the limitations of many current varieties of philosophy and social theory and that his writings provide a viable starting-point for re-imagining a new radical pedagogy against exploitation, subjugation, and oppression.

BIBLIOGRAPHIC ESSAY AND
SUGGESTED READINGS

Marcuse's unpublished papers are collected in the Stadtsbibliothek in Frankfurt Germany. Suhrkamp published a ten-volume German-language edition *Schriften* in the 1980s. Routledge has begun publishing in 1997 six volumes of unpublished material under the general editorship of Douglas Kellner, four volumes of which have appeared (see below). A German edition of the unpublished material is being published under the editorship of Peter-Erwin Jansen for zu Klampen Verlag and five volumes have appeared.

Marcuse's major works in English include:

Marcuse, H. (1941). *Reason and revolution*. New York: Oxford University Press; reprinted Boston: Beacon Press, 1960.

Marcuse, H. (1955 [1966]). *Eros and civilization*. Boston: Beacon Press.

Marcuse, H. (1958 [1988]). *Soviet Marxism*. New York: Columbia University Press.

Marcuse, H. (1964 [1991]). *One dimensional man*. Boston: Beacon Press.

Marcuse, H. (1968a). *Negations*. Boston: Beacon Press.

Marcuse, H. (1969a). *An essay on liberation*. Boston: Beacon Press.

Marcuse, H. (1969b). Revolution 1969. A conversation with Henrich von Nussbaum. *Neues Forum* XVI/181: 26-26-29.

Marcuse, H. (1970). *Five lectures*. Boston: Beacon Press.

Marcuse, H. (1972). *Counterrevolution and revolt*. Boston: Beacon Press.

Marcuse, H. (1973). *Studies in critical philosophy.* Boston: Beacon Press.

Marcuse, H. (1978). *The aesthetic dimension.* Boston: Beacon Press.

Kellner, D. editor (1998). *Technology, war and fascism: Collected papers of Herbert Marcuse Volume I*. London and New York: Routledge.

Kellner, D. editor (1998). *Toward a critical theory of society: Collected papers of Herbert Marcuse Volume II*. London and New York: Routledge.

Kellner, D. editor (2005). *The new left and the 1960s: Collected papers of Herbert Marcuse Volume III*. London and New York: Routledge.

Kellner, D. editor (2007). *Art and liberation: Collected papers of Herbert Marcuse Volume IV*. London and New York: Routledge.

FURTHER READING

Abromeit, J., and Cobb, W. M., editors (2004). *Herbert Marcuse: A critical reader*. New York: Routledge.

Alford, C. F. (1985). *Science and the revenge of nature: Marcuse and Habermas*. Gainesville: University of Florida Press.

Bokina, J., and Lukes, T. J., editors (1994). *Marcuse: New perspectives*. Lawrence, Kansas: University of Kansas Press.

Bronner, S. E., and Kellner, D. M. (1989). *Critical theory and society: A reader*. New York and London: Routledge.

Feenberg, A. (2005). *Heidegger and Marcuse: The catastrophe and redemption of history*. New York and London: Routledge.

Horkheimer, M., and Adorno, T. W. (2002). *The dialectic of enlightenment*. Stanford, CA: Stanford University Press.

Jay, M. (1996). *The dialectical imagination*. Berkeley, CA: University of California Press.

Kellner, D. (1984). *Herbert Marcuse and the crisis of Marxism*. London and Berkeley: Macmillan and University of California Press,

Pippin, R. et al., editors (1988). *Marcuse: Critical theory and the promise of utopia*. South Hadley, MA: Bergin and Garvey.

Reitz, C. (2000). *Art, alienation, and the humanities*. Albany, NY: State University of New York Press.

Schoolman, M. (1980). *The imaginary witness*. New York: Free Press.

Wiggershaus, R. (1995). *The Frankfurt School*. Cambridge, MA: MIT Press.

REFERENCES

Agamben, G. (1998). *Homo sacer: Sovereign power and bare life.* Stanford: Stanford University Press.

Beck, U. (1992). *Risk society: Towards a new modernity.* Thousand Oaks, CA: Sage Publications.

Beiser, F. (2004). A romantic education: The concept of *Bildung* in early German romanticism. In A. O. Rorty (Ed.), *Philosophers on education: New historical perspectives* (pp. 284-299). London: Routledge.

DeKoven, M. (2004). *Utopia limited: The sixties and the emergence of the postmodern.* Durham, NC: Duke University Press.

Fanon, F. (1963). *The wretched of the earth.* New York: Grove Press.

Freire, P. ([1970] 2000). *Pedagogy of the oppressed.* New York: Continuum.

Fromm, E. (1955). *The sane society.* New York: Rinehart.

Giroux, H. (2007) *The university in chains. Confronting the military-industrial-academic complex.* Boulder, CO: Paradigm Press.

Grimm, D. (2008). Philip Morris pulls the plug on controversial research program. *Science, 391,* 1173.

Harding, S. (1998). *Is science multicultural?: Postcolonialism, feminism, and epistemologies.* Bloomington, IN: Indiana University Press.

Hegel, G.W.F. (1977). *Phenomenology of spirit.* New York: Oxford University Press.

Illich, I. ([1970] 2002). *Deschooling society.* New York: Marion Boyars Publishers.

Jaeger, W. (1965 [1939]). *Paideia: The ideals of Greek culture Volume I.* New York: Oxford University Press.

Jameson, F. (1996). *Late Marxism.* London: Verso.

Kellner, D. (1989). *Critical theory, Marxism, and modernity.* Baltimore: Johns Hopkins Press.

Kellner, D., and Kahn, R. (2005). Opposite politics and the Internet: A critical/reconstructive approach. *Cultural Politics, 1*(1), 75-100.

Kellner, D., Lewis, T., Pierce, C., and Cho, D., editors (2008). *Marcuse's challenge to education.* Lanham, MA: Rowman & Littlefield.

Marcuse, H. (1976). Lecture given at Kent State April 13, 1976. Accessed through the Herbert Marcuse Archive Los Angeles February, 2007.

Marcuse, H. (1975). Lecture given at University of California, Berkeley October 18, 1975. Accessed through the Herbert Marcuse Archive Los Angeles January, 2006.

Marcuse, H. (1971). Statement on arrest of Angela Davis. Accessed through the Herbert Marcuse Archive Los Angeles January, 2006.

Marcuse, H. (1970). Lecture given at Immaculate Heart College, 1970. Accessed through the Herbert Marcuse Archive Los Angeles January, 2006.

Marcuse, H. (1968b). The responsibility of science. In L. Krieger & F. Stern (Eds.), *The responsibility of power: Historical essays in honor of Hajo Holborn* (pp. 439-444). London: Macmillian.

Marcuse, H. (1968c). Lecture given at Brooklyn College. Accessed through the Herbert Marcuse Archive Los Angeles January, 2006.

Marcuse, H. (1967). Love mystified: A critique of Norman O. Brown. *Commentary, 43*(2), 71-75.

Marcuse, H. (1966). Letter in response to SDS' educational project. Accessed through the Herbert Marcuse Archive Los Angeles January, 2006.

Schiller, F. (2004). *On the aesthetic education of man.* Mineola, NY: Dover Publications.

Zinn, H. (1999 [1980]). *A people's history of the United States 1492-present.* New York: HarperCollins Publishers.

Zizek, S. (2001). *The ticklish subject: The absent center of political ontology.* London: Verso.

Printed in the United States
By Bookmasters